Physics

Understanding the Properties of Matter and Energy

Physics

Understanding the Properties of Matter and Energy

Edited by John Murphy

Britannica®
Educational Publishing

IN ASSOCIATION WITH

ROSEN
EDUCATIONAL SERVICES

Britannica Educational Publishing in Association with Rosen Educational Services

Published in 2015 by Britannica Educational Publishing (a trademark of Encyclopædia Britannica, Inc.)
in association with The Rosen Publishing Group, Inc.
29 East 21st Street, New York, NY 10010

Distributed exclusively by Rosen Publishing.
To see additional Britannica Educational Publishing titles, go to rosenpublishing.com.

First Edition

Britannica Educational Publishing
J.E. Luebering: Director, Core Reference Group
Anthony L. Green: Editor, Compton's by Britannica

Rosen Publishing
Hope Lourie Killcoyne: Executive Editor
John Murphy: Editor
Nelson Sá: Art Director
Brian Garvey: Designer
Cindy Reiman: Photography Manager
Karen Huang: Photo Researcher
Introduction and supplementary material by Tracey Baptiste

Library of Congress Cataloging-in-Publication Data

Physics: understanding the properties of matter and energy/edited by John Murphy.—(First edition.
    pages cm.—(The study of science)
Includes bibliographical references and index.
Audience: Grades 7 to 12.
ISBN 978-1-62275-418-2 (library bound)
1. Matter—(Properties—(Juvenile literature. 2. Force and energy—(Juvenile literature. 3. Physics—
(Juvenile literature. I. Murphy, John, 1968– editor.
QC173.36. P49 2015
530—(dc23

                                                                              2014006452

Manufactured in the United States of America

CONTENTS

Matter and energy are the basic building blocks of the universe. Matter is anything that has mass and occupies space. It is made up of particles called atoms and molecules, which means that this book you are holding, the water you drink, and even the air you breathe have mass. Even though atoms have mass, most of an atom is actually empty space. An atom is made of electrons, protons, and neutrons. The mass of an atom is centered in its nucleus, where different numbers of protons and neutrons are combined, forming a variety of chemical elements. Molecules are groups of two or more atoms. The most familiar states of matter are solid, liquid, and gas, but there is a fourth: plasma.

Energy is defined as the capacity for doing work. In the early 1900s, Albert Einstein theorized that energy and matter are related to each other in a fundamental way. He proposed that it was possible to convert matter into energy. His theories helped scientists understand nuclear energy. Einstein also understood that the reverse was possible, converting energy into matter, though this is difficult to achieve because of the large amounts of energy that are needed.

Energy can be categorized into two basic types: kinetic and potential. Kinetic energy is energy of

This girl and the skateboard she is on are made of matter, and they are demonstrating kinetic energy—the energy of matter in motion. Purestock/Thinkstock

motion. A bird flying through the air and an arrow shot out of a bow both have kinetic energy. Potential energy is energy that is stored up but not yet used. A rubber band that has been stretched out has potential energy. As soon as it is let go, that energy becomes kinetic because it is in motion. The water behind a dam also has potential energy, which becomes kinetic energy when water released from a dam rushes out.

In this book, you will learn about the fundamentals of matter and energy, and how physicists have discovered the basic building blocks of the universe and their properties. You will also learn about the prominent scientists who have made these discoveries, tested theories, and given us a wider view of the known universe, all by looking at its most basic parts.

CHAPTER 1

WHAT IS MATTER?

A n electron, a grain of sand, an elephant, and a giant quasar at the edge of the visible universe all have one thing in common: they are composed of matter. Matter is the material substance that makes up the physical universe. A beam of light, the motion of a falling stone,

Large elephants and the tiny dust specs that they kick up are all made of the same substance—matter. Johan Swanepoel/Shutterstock.com

and the explosion of a stick of dynamite all have one thing in common: they are expressions of energy. Energy and matter together form the basis for all observable phenomena.

THE STATES OF MATTER

Most of the matter that people ordinarily observe can be classified into one of three states, or phases: solid, liquid, or gas. Solid

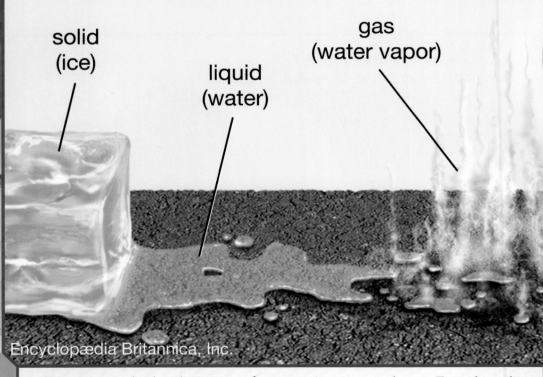

Water exists in the three basic states of matter as ice, water, and vapor. Encyclopædia Britannica, Inc.

matter generally possesses and retains a definite size and shape, no matter where it is situated. A pencil, for example, does not change in size or shape if it is moved from a desktop and placed upright in a glass. A liquid, unlike a solid, assumes the shape of its container, even though, like a solid, it has a definite size, or volume. A pint of water changes its shape when it is poured from a glass into a bowl, but its volume remains the same. A gas expands to fill the complete volume of its container.

At a given temperature and pressure, a substance will be in the solid, liquid, or gaseous state. But if the temperature or the pressure changes, its state may also change. At constant atmospheric pressure, the state of water, for example, changes with changes in temperature. Ice is water in a solid state. If it is removed from a freezer and placed in a warm pan, the ice warms up and changes to a liquid: water. If the pan is then placed over a hot fire, the water heats up and changes to the gaseous state: steam.

Most substances can exist in any of the three states, provided that they do not decompose chemically, as sugar, for example, often does when it is heated in air. Oxygen must be cooled to very low temperatures before it becomes a liquid or a solid. Quartz must be

heated to very high temperatures before it becomes a liquid or a gas.

In most people's experience, wide changes in pressure are not as common as drastic changes in temperature. For this reason, examples of the effects of pressure on the states of matter are not common. Often high-pressure machines and vacuum (low-pressure) machines must be used to study the effects of pressure changes on matter. Under very low pressures, matter generally tends to enter the gaseous phase. At very high pressures, gases tend to liquefy and liquids tend to solidify. In fact, at the very lowest temperatures that can be reached, helium will not solidify unless a pressure of some 25 times the normal atmospheric pressure is applied.

The relation between pressure and temperature in changes of state is familiar to people who live at high altitudes. There, the pressure is lower than at sea level, so water boils at a lower temperature. Cooking anything in water takes longer on a mountaintop than at sea level.

These properties of the three states of matter are easily observed. They are explained, however, by a theory that describes the behavior of particles far too small to be seen.

ATOMIC THEORY OF MATTER

All substances are made up of tiny units called atoms. Each atom consists of a massive, positively charged center called the nucleus, around which fly one or more negatively charged electrons.

The nucleus itself contains at least one proton, a positively charged particle. In all atoms, except those of ordinary hydrogen, the nucleus also contains at least one neutron, a particle that has no electrical

Hydrogen Atom   **Oxygen Atom**

One electron (pink) circles the lone proton (blue) in a hydrogen atom. An oxygen atom has eight protons (blue), which can bind eight electrons. Encyclopædia Britannica, Inc.

charge. A neutral atom has the same number of electrons as protons, so the electrical charges cancel.

The identity of an atom and its atomic number is determined by the number of protons in its nucleus. For example, there is one proton in the nucleus of a hydrogen atom, so hydrogen has the atomic number 1. Oxygen, with eight protons, has the atomic number 8; iron has the atomic number 26; and mercury has the atomic number 80.

Substances that are composed of only one kind of atom are called elements. Only 90 elements occur naturally on Earth in significant amounts. The lightest is hydrogen; the heaviest is uranium.

The nuclei of a given element all have the same number of protons but may have a differing number of neutrons. For example, about 99.8 percent of the oxygen nuclei in nature contain eight neutrons as well as eight protons. But a very few oxygen nuclei contain nine neutrons, and some even contain ten neutrons. Each kind of nucleus is a different isotope of oxygen. Each isotope has a different number of neutrons.

Most hydrogen atoms are made up of a single proton with an electron circling it.

However, one isotope of hydrogen contains a single neutron as well. This isotope is called deuterium. Because neutrons have approximately the same mass as protons, deuterium atoms have about twice as much mass as those of the ordinary isotope of hydrogen. An extremely rare form of hydrogen, called tritium, has one proton and two neutrons in its nucleus. This is an unstable arrangement, so the tritium nucleus is radioactive. Over time, it gives off a negatively charged particle and changes to a stable helium nucleus with two protons and one neutron.

THREE OXYGEN ISOTOPES

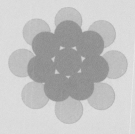
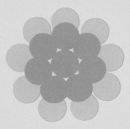

oxygen 16   oxygen 17   oxygen 18

This diagram represents the nuclei of three oxygen isotopes. Each nucleus has eight protons (gray) and eight, nine, or ten neutrons (green). Encyclopædia Britannica, Inc.

Many other isotopes of the various elements are radioactive. They can give off radiation of different kinds, changing to other elements or to different isotopes of the same element. Many radioactive isotopes are human-made, produced in nuclear reactors and particle accelerators.

The heaviest element that occurs in significant amounts in nature, uranium, has 92 protons, and its most common isotope has 146 neutrons. Transuranium elements—elements with more protons than uranium—are relatively unstable. Some exist for only a fraction of a second before they decay into other elements. Scientists have synthesized about two dozen of these transuranium elements, a few of which were later found to occur naturally in trace amounts in uranium ores.

Substances that are composed of more than one kind of atom are either compounds or mixtures. The atoms in compounds are joined together chemically. In one type of compound, ions (electrically charged atoms or groups of atoms) are held together; in another type of compound, atoms are joined together to form molecules. This chemical bonding is the result of the electrical forces between the ions or the force of attraction of the electrons of one atom for the nucleus of another atom. For example, in one type of bonding, two atoms of hydrogen and one atom of oxygen share electrons and form a water molecule. The chemical symbol for water, H_2O, denotes this combination.

The atoms, ions, or molecules in a mixture intermingle with one another but are not joined chemically. Salt water is a kind of mixture called a solution. Salt is composed of ions, and they spread throughout the water when the salt dissolves.

Regardless of whether water is in the solid, liquid, or gaseous state, its molecules always consist of one atom of oxygen and two atoms of hydrogen. Solid water, liquid water, and gaseous water all have the same chemical composition. Instead, the difference between these physical states depends on which energy is larger: the energy associated with the attraction between molecules or the heat energy.

ATOMIC THEORY AND THE STATES OF MATTER

A certain amount of attraction exists between all molecules. If repulsive forces are weaker than these intermolecular attractive forces, the molecules stick together. However,

molecules are in constant random motion because of their thermal, or heat, energy. As the temperature of a substance increases, this molecular motion becomes greater. The molecules spread out and are less likely to unite. As the temperature decreases, the motion becomes smaller. The molecules are thus more likely to linger in each other's vicinity and bind together.

In a solid, the intermolecular attractive forces overcome the disruptive thermal energies of the molecules. In most solids, the molecules are bound together in a rigid, orderly arrangement called a crystal. These types of solids are called crystalline solids. (In some other solids, such as glasses, gels, and many plastics, the molecules are not arranged in crystals.) Although the molecules in a crystal are held rigidly in place, they still vibrate because of their thermal energy. It may be difficult to think of ice as having heat energy. But even in ice, each water molecule, though held firmly in the crystal pattern, vibrates around a fixed position. This vibrational motion is an expression of the thermal energy of ice.

As the temperature of the solid is increased, its molecules vibrate with greater and greater energy until they gain enough vibrational energy to overcome the intermolecular attractive forces. They then break loose from their fixed positions in the crystal arrangement and move about more or less freely. The substance now assumes the shape of its container but maintains a constant volume. In other words, the substance has melted and is now a liquid.

Melting is a change of state, or a phase change. The temperature at which melting takes place varies from substance to substance. Water and iron, for example, melt at different temperatures. The melting temperature is the same, however, for a given material at a given pressure. At atmospheric pressure, water always melts at 32 °F (0 °C).

Phase changes can work in reverse. If the temperature of a liquid is gradually decreased, a point is eventually reached at which the intermolecular forces are strong enough to bind the molecules despite the disruptive thermal motions. Then a crystal forms: the substance has frozen. The temperature at which this liquid-to-solid phase change takes place is the freezing point. The freezing point of a substance occurs at the same temperature as its melting point. This is true for all substances that are crystals in their solid form.

This theory of matter can also explain the liquid-to-gas change of state, a process called vaporization or evaporation. As heat is applied

THE FOURTH STATE OF MATTER

At extremely high temperatures, atoms may collide with such force that electrons are knocked free from the nuclei. The resulting mixture of free negative and positive particles is not a gas, according to the usual definition. Such material is called plasma. Some scientists consider the plasma state to be a fourth state of matter. Actually, about 99 percent of the known matter in the universe is in the plasma state. Plasmas possess remarkable properties not found in ordinary solids, liquids, and gases. Because the free electrons are extremely mobile, for example, plasmas are excellent conductors of heat and electricity.

Physical states

increasing energy

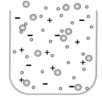

Solid

The molecules that make up a solid are arranged in regular, repeating patterns. They are held firmly in place but can vibrate within a limited area.

Liquid

The molecules that make up a liquid flow easily around one another. They are kept from flying apart by attractive forces between them. Liquids assume the shape of their containers.

Gas

The molecules that make up a gas fly in all directions at great speeds. They are so far apart that the attractive forces between them are insignificant.

Plasma

At the very high temperatures of stars, atoms lose their electrons. The mixture of electrons and nuclei that results is the plasma state of matter.

to a liquid, some molecules gain sufficient thermal energy to overcome the intermolecular attraction—surface tension—exerted by molecules at the surface of the liquid. These high-energy molecules break free from the liquid and move away. Such molecules are now in the gaseous state. As more heat is applied, more molecules gain enough energy to move away until—at a temperature called the boiling point of the liquid—all the molecules can gain enough energy to escape from the liquid state.

The average distance between molecules in the gaseous state is extremely large compared to the size of the molecules, so the intermolecular forces in a gas are quite weak. This explains why a gas fills the entire volume of its container. Since intermolecular forces are so small, a gas molecule moves until it strikes either another gas molecule or the container wall. The net effect of the many molecules striking the container walls is observed as pressure.

Sometimes a substance will pass directly from the solid state to the gaseous state without passing through the liquid state. This process is called sublimation. Dry ice (solid carbon dioxide) sublimates at atmospheric pressure. Liquid carbon dioxide can form if the gas is subjected to more than five times the atmospheric pressure.

INERTIA AND GRAVITATION

Another way of approaching the subject of matter is based on the concepts of inertia and gravitation. Matter can be defined as anything that has inertia and that experiences an attractive force when in a gravitational field.

INERTIA

Isaac Newton's first law of motion describes inertia. A body at rest tends to remain at rest; a body in motion tends to keep on moving at the same speed and in a straight line. In order to move a resting body or stop a moving body, some effort, called a force, is required. The tendency of a body to remain at rest or, once moving, to remain in motion is inertia.

The inertia of a body is related to its mass. More massive bodies possess greater inertia than less massive bodies. A body's mass can be measured by exerting a force on the body and observing the acceleration that results. Newton's second law of motion states that the mass (m) is equal to the force (F) divided by the acceleration (a): $m = F/a$.

In principle, this measurement can be made anywhere in the universe. Wherever the experiment is performed, the same force applied to the same body produces the same acceleration. The mass of a body is, therefore, the same everywhere. (According to relativity, a moving body's mass actually increases with its speed, as will be discussed below. However, at all but extremely high speeds—those approaching the speed of light—this change in mass is too tiny to be observed.)

GRAVITATION

All matter exerts a gravitational attractive force on other matter. The gravitational force is weak compared to the three other known forces: the electromagnetic force, the strong force (which holds the nucleus of an atom together), and the weak force (which is involved in some forms of radio-activity). The magnetic force of a small magnet, for example, can hold up a pin against the gravitational pull of the entire Earth. However, on the scale of everyday objects near Earth or that of astronomical bodies, the gravitational force is the domi-nant one of the four known forces. The fall of bodies released from a height to the sur-face of Earth is the most familiar example of gravitation. Earth's orbit around the Sun

and the motion of the sun are also results of the force of gravitation.

The weight of a body is determined by the gravitational forces exerted upon it. A body at Earth's surface experiences a gravitational pull toward the center of the planet. If the body moves farther from Earth's center (to the top of a high mountain, for example), the gravitational force on it decreases, so its weight decreases. If the body moves to a lower point on Earth's surface (into a deep valley, for example), the gravitational force on it increases, so its weight increases. The increase is far greater if the body then moves to the gravitational field of a giant planet, say, Jupiter. A body's weight can change; it varies with the strength of the gravitational field in which the body is placed.

It is important to understand the difference between mass and weight. Although the mass of a body is the same everywhere, the weight of a body depends on the strength of the local gravitational field. An astronaut standing on the surface of the moon weighs less than when standing on Earth, but the astronaut's mass is the same in both places.

Nevertheless, there is a relationship between mass and weight. Mass and weight are proportional to each other. The more mass a body has, the more it will weigh at any given point in space.

THE BUILDING BLOCKS OF MATTER

All matter is made up of elementary particles. Atoms are not elementary particles, since they are themselves composed of smaller particles: electrons, protons, and neutrons. Some particles, such as photons, commonly exist apart from atoms.

As scientists developed methods for studying radioactive particles, breaking atoms apart, and detecting particles from space (cosmic rays), they concluded that other particles in addition to the photon, electron, proton, and neutron must exist. In the early 1930s, Wolfgang Pauli and Enrico Fermi postulated the neutrino, a particle with no charge and either very little or no mass that interacts much more weakly with matter than a photon does. They held that only the existence of such a particle could account for the energy and momentum that are lost when a neutron in a nucleus decays into a proton and a free electron, a process called beta decay. Particles with the characteristics postulated by Pauli and Fermi were very difficult to detect, but

experiments performed in 1956 confirmed their existence.

Since then, hundreds of different particles have been detected as a result of collisions produced in cosmic-ray reactions and particle-accelerator experiments. They are called subatomic particles because they are smaller than an atom. Most of these particles are highly unstable, existing for less than a millionth of a second. There are three different types of sub-atomic particle: leptons, quarks, and bosons. Leptons and quarks together form atoms, so they are considered the basic building blocks of matter. The six known types of leptons are the electron, the muon, the tau, and the three types of neutrino. There are also six types of quark. Quarks make up neutrons and protons. Bosons include the photon (seen as light), the graviton, and the gluon. The graviton is a theoretical particle that has not yet been dis-covered. If it exists, the graviton carries the gravitational force, just as the photon carries the electromagnetic force and the gluon car-ries the strong force.

ANTIMATTER

In 1928, P. A. M. Dirac claimed that a particle of the same mass as an electron but having a positive charge could exist. Four years later, a positive electron, or positron, was detected. This was the first experimental evidence for the existence of antimatter. If a particle possesses an electrical charge, its antiparticle possesses an equal but opposite charge. Many other kinds of antimatter particles have since been discovered. Particle physicists now assume that for every type of subatomic particle that occurs in nature, a corresponding antiparticle exists, even if the antiparticle has not been observed. A specific type of antiparticle may be discovered years after its corresponding particle. Scientists have also created antiatoms, which are made up of antiparticles.

An important property of matter is demonstrated when an electron and a positron meet. They annihilate one another. Both particles disappear. According to the law of conservation of mass-energy, if mass is destroyed, an equivalent amount of energy must be created. So the sum of mass-energy before and after annihilation is exactly equal.

This is precisely what happens. When an electron and a positron annihilate each other, a large amount of energy, corresponding to the mass of the two particles, is always given off. Similar annihilations occur when other particles meet their antiparticles.

A converse to the process of particle-antiparticle annihilation is known as pair production, in which radiation disappears and matter is created. The most common example is the creation of an electron-positron pair from a photon. For this to occur, a minimum photon energy, corresponding to two electron masses, is necessary.

The Milky Way galaxy, to which Earth belongs, is apparently composed primarily of particles rather than antiparticles. It obviously cannot be made up of equal amounts of particles and antiparticles, for if it were, there would be a cataclysmic annihilation and the matter in the galaxy would be converted to radiation. There is also no evidence that other galaxies in the universe are composed primarily of antiparticles. Matter apparently dominates antimatter in the universe.

CHAPTER 2

FORCE AND MOTION

A force is an action that changes or maintains the motion of a body or object. Simply stated, a force is a push or a pull. Forces can change an object's speed, its direction, and even its shape. Pushing a door open, pulling it closed, stretching a rubber band—all of these actions require force.

Force is a vector quantity—that is, it has both magnitude (size) and direction. Although forces cannot be seen directly, their effects can be observed and measured. Force is measured using an instrument called a force meter. The unit of measurement for force is the newton, symbolized by the letter N and named in honor of the English physicist Isaac Newton. Much of what is known today about force is based on Newton's three fundamental laws of motion.

BALANCED AND UNBALANCED FORCES

Knowing the size and direction of the forces acting on an object allows you to predict how its motion will change. The combination of all the forces acting on an object simultaneously is called the net force, also known as the resultant force. For example, the net force acting on a rope being pulled from the right by a force of five newtons and from the left by a force of three newtons will be two newtons pulling from the right.

When the forces applied to an object are balanced, the net force is equal to zero and the motion of the object will not change. If the object is at rest, it will remain at rest. If it is moving, it

Newton's laws of motion

net force = 0

F = 200 N

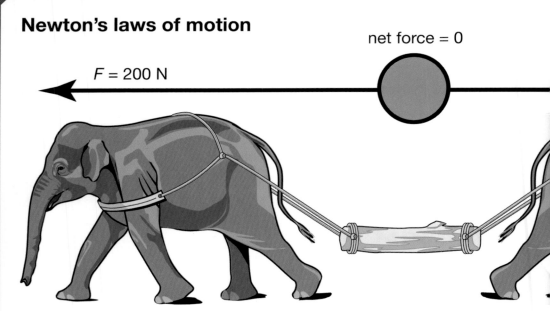

When an object is acted on by equal and opposite forces, it is at rest. Encyclopædia Britannica, Inc.

will continue to move with the same velocity—at the same speed and in the same direction. Like force, velocity is a vector quantity; it is measured in units of meters traveled per second (m/s).

When the forces applied to an object are unbalanced, the net force is not equal to zero. Unbalanced forces will change the velocity of the object—it will speed up, slow down, or change direction. The motion of the rope in the example given above is the result of unbalanced forces.

These observations about force and motion are supported by Newton's first law of motion. The law states that an object at rest will remain at rest, and an object in motion will remain in motion with the same velocity unless the object is acted upon by an unbalanced force. In formulating this law, Newton was greatly influenced by the work of the Italian scientist Galileo. From his studies of the

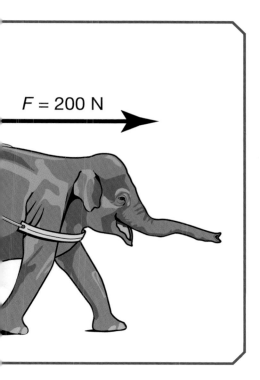

$F = 200$ N

motion of falling objects, Galileo had deduced that a body in motion would remain in motion unless a force caused it to come to rest.

Newton's first law is sometimes called the law of inertia. Inertia is the resistance of an

NEWTON'S MONUMENTAL CONTRIBUTIONS

In the year Galileo died (1642), there was born in England one of the greatest scientists of all time, Isaac Newton. His experiments with light laid the foundation for the modern science of optics. He also built the world's first reflecting telescope (a telescope that uses mirrors to focus light). His studies of falling bodies and of the solar system led to his celebrated law of universal gravitation.

Newton developed a special mathematics for treating problems in mechanics. Thus he became one of the discoverers of calculus. The other was Gottfried Wilhelm Leibniz. Newton provided firm bases for expressing natural laws as mathematical formulas. His method started with locating objects in space with measurements made to three axes at right angles to each other through a chosen point called the origin. Such measurements are called Cartesian coordinates after René Descartes, who devised them.

Newton also discovered many of the basic laws of mechanics, including the three fundamental laws of motion, which he published in 1687. These laws describe the relations between the forces (pushes or pulls) acting on an object and the motion of the object.

object to a change in its speed or direction. The greater an object's mass, the greater its inertia, and the greater the force needed to change its motion. For example, it is harder to lift a backpack full of books than it is to lift an empty backpack. The full backpack has more inertia than the empty backpack because it has more mass, so more force is needed to move it. Inertia is a fundamental property of all matter.

FORCE, MASS, AND ACCELERATION

Unbalanced forces acting on an object will cause it to accelerate, or change its motion, in the direction of the applied force. Acceleration is a vector quantity defined as a change in velocity over time; it is measured as meters traveled per second per second, or meters per second squared (m/s^2).

The acceleration of an object depends on two things: the object's mass and the size of the applied force. The greater the force applied to an object, the more that object will accelerate; the greater the mass of an object, the less that object will accelerate. For example, a wagon pulled by a large dog will have a greater acceleration than will the same wagon

pulled by a small dog. This is because the large dog applies more force to the wagon than the small dog applies. More force means greater acceleration if the object's mass is the same. If you fill the large dog's wagon with sand, the wagon will have a smaller acceleration than it did when it was empty. This is because the sand-filled wagon has more mass than the empty wagon. More mass means less acceleration if the applied force is the same.

The relationship between force, mass, and acceleration forms the basis of Newton's second law of motion. The law states that the acceleration of an object increases with increased force, decreases with increased mass, and occurs in the direction of the net force being applied.

Newton described the relationship between force, mass, and acceleration mathematically in the formula:

Force = mass × acceleration

This is more commonly expressed as:

F = ma

Force is expressed in units of newtons (N), mass is measured in kilograms (kg), and acceleration is measured as meters per second per second, or meters per second squared (m/s²). Therefore, force is measured in units of mass times units of acceleration:

$$\text{Force (N)} = \text{mass (kg)} \times \text{acceleration (m/s}^2\text{)}$$

Because force is expressed in units of newtons, one newton (1 N) is the amount of force needed to accelerate one kilogram (1 kg) of mass at the rate of one meter per second per second (1 m/s²):

$$1 \text{ N} = 1 \text{ kg} \cdot \text{m/s}^2$$

Newton's second law of motion can also be applied to an object moving in a circle. If force is exerted at a right angle to the direction in which the object is moving, the object will turn. If force continues to be applied at a right angle to the direction of the object as it turns, it will keep turning and will move in a circle. The force that keeps an object moving in a circle is called centripetal force. Centripetal force always points toward the center of a circle. If you whirl an object on a string, you are applying a centripetal force on the object. The

INVERCHARRON

The end of this athlete's hammer (during the Invercharron Highland Games) experiences centripetal force along the pole toward the center of the circle, where the athlete is standing. Ian MacNicol/Getty Images

direction of the centripetal force is toward your hand at the center of the circle.

Following Newton's law of $F = ma$, you can increase the whirling object's acceleration by increasing the amount of centripetal force—that is, by pulling harder on the string. If you use the same amount of force to whirl a heavier object, its acceleration will decrease and it will move more slowly. Note that it is the centripetal force you are applying that keeps the object moving in a circle. If you let go of the string, the object continues moving, but not in a circle—it will travel in a straight line in the direction it was headed when you let go.

ACTION AND REACTION FORCES

All forces act in pairs. If an object pushes (or pulls) another object, the second object pushes (or pulls) the first object in the opposite direction with an equal amount of force. For example, if you lean on a wall, you exert a force on the wall, and the wall exerts an equal force back on you. The weight of a table exerts a force downward against the floor; the floor exerts an equal amount of force upward against the table.

Such observations form the basis of Newton's third law of motion, which describes

how forces behave when two bodies interact. The law states that for every force, there is a reaction force that is equal in size but opposite in direction. That is, when an object exerts a force on another object, the second object exerts an equal and opposite force on the first object. These "force pairs" are sometimes referred to as action and reaction forces.

Although action and reaction forces are equal and opposite, they should not be confused with balanced forces. Balanced forces are equal and opposite forces that act on a single object. Because of this, balanced forces cancel each other out, so there is no change in the motion of the object. Action and reaction forces are equal and opposite forces that act on different objects. Action and reaction forces do not cancel each other out and often result in motion.

KINDS OF FORCES

Forces can be divided into two main categories: contact forces and field forces.

CONTACT FORCES

Contact forces are forces in which two or more objects or bodies touch or contact each other directly. There are many kinds of contact forces. Among the most familiar are friction, air resistance, and elastic forces.

FRICTION

Friction is a force that resists motion between two surfaces that are in contact with each other. When you walk, the frictional force between the ground and the soles of your shoes resists your forward motion. Friction works in opposition to

The resistance of motion between the match and the surface creates friction, which then creates a spark. KConstantine/Shutterstock.com

the direction of an object's motion. If you push a chair, you apply a force to move it forward. The floor exerts a frictional force in the opposite direction—toward you—to resist the forward motion of the chair.

Friction is much greater on rough surfaces than it is on smooth surfaces. For example, it is easier to glide across ice wearing metal skates than it is wearing rubber boots because the friction between metal and ice is less than the friction between ice and rubber.

Frictional forces can be helpful or unhelpful. For example, friction between rubber tires and the road helps the tires resist sliding. Friction between brakes and the wheels of a car or bicycle helps the vehicles slow down. However, failing to keep a bike chain lubricated can increase friction between the chain and axel, making the bike harder to pedal.

Friction between surfaces generates heat. When you rub your hands together, friction between your hands produces heat, causing your hands to warm up. However, heat produced by the friction between moving machine parts can cause serious damage. To counter this, lubricants such as oil are used to reduce friction between moving parts of a machine and prevent damage from overheating.

AIR RESISTANCE

Air resistance is the frictional force that air exerts against a moving object. As an object moves, air resistance slows it down. The faster the object's motion, the greater the air resistance exerted against it. Air resistance affects all moving objects, from airplanes, rockets, and trains to cars, bicycles, and even living things.

An object's shape and surface area can increase or decrease the degree of air resistance it encounters. A feather will fall more slowly than a metal ball because the feather has a greater surface area. Because it can spread its weight over a larger area, the feather encounters greater air resistance and falls more slowly. This is the principle used in the parachute.

Streamlining helps decrease air resistance. This is demonstrated by the smooth curved shapes of planes, modern

The large surface of a parachute increases the amount of air resistance the skydiver encounters, allowing for a slower descent to the ground. Ivica Drusany/Shutterstock.com

cars, and high-speed trains, which greatly decrease the effect of air resistance, allowing these vehicles to travel more efficiently. Bicycle racers crouch low on their bikes—and joggers run with elbows tucked in—to reduce the effect of air resistance.

ELASTIC FORCES

Some forces can affect an object's shape. If you pull the ends of a rubber band, it stretches and simultaneously resists being stretched. The resistance comes from forces between the particles in the rubber band. Similarly, if you squeeze a ball of clay, forces between particles in the clay resist being pushed together. The forces that an object exerts to resist a change in its shape are called elastic forces; they are transferred through the particles that comprise materials. Two types of elastic forces are tension and compression.

Tension is the elastic force that stretches or pulls an object. If you loop a short length of thread through a metal ring and let the ring hang by the thread, the force of gravity will pull the ring downward. The ring does not fall to the ground, however, because tension forces between the particles in the thread pull the rope upward. Tension forces apply only when an object is being pulled or stretched. If you let go of the thread, gravity will pull it (and the metal ring) to the ground. The thread will no longer have tension because it is not being stretched.

Compression is the elastic force that squeezes or pushes an object. If you squeeze a metal spring, the force from your fingers will push the particles in the spring closer together; at the same time, the particles will resist being pushed together and will push back against your fingers.

Elastic forces are also exerted by a surface when an object is pressing against it. A book resting on a table experiences a downward pull from the force of gravity. However, the book does not fall through the table because the table exerts an upward compressive force against the book. The book remains at rest because the forces on the book (gravity from Earth pulling downward and compression from the table pushing upward) are balanced and cancel each other out, following Newton's first law of motion.

FIELD FORCES

Field forces are those forces in which bodies interact without directly touching each other. They are also referred to as noncontact forces

or at-a-distance forces. There are four types of field forces: gravity, electromagnetic forces, and the strong force and the weak force found in atoms. These four forces comprise the most fundamental forces in the universe.

GRAVITY

Gravity, or gravitational force, is the force of attraction between matter. A dropped object falls to the ground because it is pulled down by the gravitational force exerted by Earth. Gravity is the force that holds Earth, the Sun, and the stars together and keeps the planets in their orbits.

Gravity is affected by mass and distance. The force of gravity between two objects increases as their respective masses increase and decreases as the distance between them increases. Simply put, the larger the objects are, the greater the attraction between them; the farther they are from each other, the less their mutual attraction. These two principles were summarized by Newton in his law of universal gravitation. In the 20th century, Albert Einstein added to our understanding of gravity with his general theory of relativity.

Of the four fundamental forces, gravity is the weakest. Gravity is further distinguished from the other forces in that it is universally attractive—that is, it acts between any two objects in the universe—and because it acts over an infinite distance.

ELECTROMAGNETIC FORCES

Electromagnetic forces are the forces of electricity and of magnetism. Electricity and magnetism were long thought to be separate forces. A number of discoveries in the 19th century showed that both are aspects

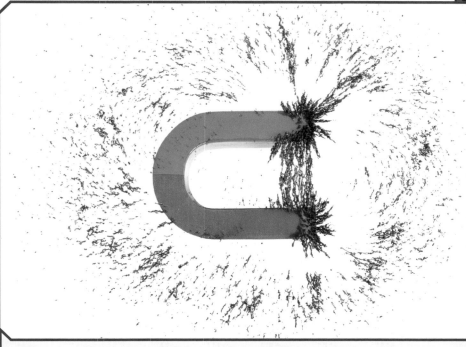

This magnet and iron filings show lines of attraction and repulsion. Lines of force between oppositely charged point charges (red and blue) merge toward each other. MilanB/Shutterstock.com

of a common phenomenon. Electromagnetic forces are among the strongest of the fundamental forces and are far stronger than the force of gravity.

Electromagnetic forces are caused by electromagnetic fields. A field is a region that extends outward from a charged object. Fields can exist in space far from the charge that generated them. However, electric and magnetic fields are not infinite in size and can cancel out over long distances.

Unlike gravitation, electromagnetic forces can both attract and repel. An electric force exists between any two charged objects. The objects attract each other if they carry opposite charges (one is negatively charged, and one is positively charged). The objects repel each other if they carry like charges (both are positively charged, or both are negatively charged). The strength of the electric force between two charged objects depends on the size of the charges and the distance between objects. The greater the charge, the stronger the force; the greater the distance between the objects, the weaker the force between them.

Magnetic forces are similar to electric forces. However, magnetic forces only attract or repel electrically charged particles that are in motion, whereas electric forces act on any charged particles—whether they are moving or stationary. Magnetic forces also act on certain materials, such as iron.

STRONG AND WEAK NUCLEAR FORCES

The strong force and the weak force both operate inside the nuclei of atoms. The strong force is the strongest force in the universe and has the shortest range. The strong force acts to hold the protons and neutrons together inside the nucleus of an atom. Neutrons carry no charge, but protons are positively charged. All elements except hydrogen carry more than one proton and therefore carry more than one positive charge. Because like-charged particles repel each other, the strong force must be strong enough to overcome this repulsion and hold these particles together inside the atomic nucleus.

The weak force is responsible for emitting certain types of subatomic particles during radioactive decay. It also helps initiate the nuclear fusion reaction that fuels the sun. The weak force is weaker than the strong force and electromagnetic forces but far stronger than gravity.

CHAPTER 3

WHAT IS ENERGY?

A rock falling off a cliff is different from the same rock lying on the ground below. A rubber band pulled taut is different from the same rubber band left slack. A glowing lightbulb is different from the same bulb when the electricity is switched off. It is the same rock, the same rubber band, and the same lightbulb. The difference is one of energy.

Energy is one of the most basic ideas of science. All activity in the universe can be explained in terms of energy and matter. But the definition of energy is not at all simple, since energy occurs in many different forms. It is not always easy to tell how these forms are related to one another and what they have in common. One of the best-known definitions of energy is the classical definition used in physics: energy is the ability to do work.

Physicists define work in a way that does not always agree with the average person's idea of work. In physics, work is done when a force applied to an object moves it some distance in the direction of the force.

Mathematically, $W = Fs$, where W is the work done, F is the force applied, and s is the distance moved. If either F or s is equal to zero, W is also equal to zero, so no work is done.

When an old man walks up a long flight of stairs, he may regard it as work—he exerts effort to move his body to a higher level. In this instance, he also does work according to the definition accepted by physicists, for he exerts a force to lift himself over a distance—the distance from the bottom to the top of the stairs.

The experimental detonation of an atomic bomb on Enewetak atoll in 1952 was a vivid demonstration of nuclear energy—the energy contained in the atomic nucleus. United States Department of Energy

However, a young man who holds a heavy weight in his outstretched arms without moving is not doing any work as physicists define work. He is exerting a force that keeps the weight from falling to the floor, but the position of the weight remains unchanged. It is not moved any distance by the force. The person is, of course, exerting considerable muscular effort to avoid dropping the weight, and the average person would say that he is working very hard indeed. But he is not doing any work according to the definition accepted in physics.

ENERGY SYSTEMS

Energy is readily transferred from object to object, especially in the form of heat. For this reason, it is often necessary to study an entire group of objects that may be transferring energy back and forth among themselves. Such a group is called a system. The energy of a system is the ability of the entire system to do work. If the parts of a system do work on one another but do not change anything outside the system, then the total amount of energy in the system stays the same. However, the amount of energy in one part of the system may decrease and

the amount of energy of another part may increase.

Consider a system consisting of a rainforest with many trees, a vine hanging from the central tree, the ground supporting the trees, and a monkey standing beneath the tree from which the vine is hanging. The monkey, holding the free end of the vine, climbs up the central tree. It then moves several treetops away, maintaining the same altitude.

Finally, the monkey grasps the vine that is still tied to the central tree and swings down, past the central tree, and up again until it lands in a third tree. An observer watching the monkey swinging from one tree to the other will conclude that the system possesses energy and can do work.

The necessary elements in this system are the monkey, the trees, Earth, and the vine. The monkey provides the initial energy by climbing the trees, while the trees support the monkey against the force of gravity, which pulls downward. Earth's gravitational attraction is the force that draws the monkey downward once it begins to swing on the vine. The vine supports the monkey so that it remains free to then swing upward against the force of gravity and into another tree. When all these elements occur together, the system is capable of doing work; it has energy.

KINETIC AND POTENTIAL ENERGY

When the monkey swings on the vine, it is acting like a pendulum. Like any pendulum, it is exhibiting the difference between two kinds of energy: kinetic and potential.

Kinetic energy is the energy of motion. While the monkey is swinging from one tree to the other, it has kinetic energy. So, too, does a speeding bus, a falling raindrop, and a spinning top. Any moving object has this type of energy.

Potential energy is the energy an object or system has because of the position of its parts. It is often thought of as "stored" energy (though it is important to remember that energy is not a substance). For example, a stretched spring has potential energy. Force has been applied to stretch the spring, creating stored energy. The more the spring is stretched from its normal position, the greater its capacity to do work when released. Likewise, a metal weight has more potential energy raised above the ground than it has after falling to Earth. In the raised position, it is capable of doing more work because of the pull of gravity.

The monkey also has potential energy as it stands in the treetop. The monkey is not moving, so it has no kinetic energy. But the system has energy because of the monkey's location above the ground. The work done to lift the monkey against the force of gravity has created potential energy.

The potential energy is released when the monkey jumps off the tree. Gravity pulls it downward, and it travels faster and faster until, as it sweeps by the ground, it is traveling very fast. In place of the lost potential energy, the system has gained more and more kinetic energy. When the monkey lands in the next tree, the system again has potential energy but no kinetic energy.

This example demonstrates a basic property of energy—it can manifest itself in different ways. In this case, potential energy was converted to kinetic energy, which was then changed back into potential energy.

MECHANICAL ENERGY

The term "mechanical energy" can be applied to systems in which all the significant components (such as the monkey, trees, Earth, and vine) are visible to the naked eye. Mechanical energy is equal to kinetic energy, plus potential energy. It is thus all the energy an object has because of its motion and its position. Machines—from

CONSERVATION OF ENERGY

One of the most important ideas in physics is known as the law of conservation of energy. It states that energy cannot be created or destroyed. It can be changed from one form to another, but in an isolated system—that is, a system with no outside forces acting on it—the total amount of energy never changes. For example, a falling object has a constant amount of energy, but the energy of the object changes from potential to kinetic.

Another example of this law is the collision of a moving object with another moving object or a stationary object. If after the collision both objects are moving, the initial kinetic energy of the first object equals the total kinetic energy of the two objects after the collision, plus any sound and heat energy formed during the collision.

With the introduction of the special theory of relativity in 1905, mass was recognized as equivalent to energy. This means that energy can be converted to mass, and vice versa. In nuclear reactions, the high-speed particles experience a significant increase in their mass as a result of their great energy. To account for such reactions, the laws of conservation of energy and conservation of mass have been combined into one conservation law: the law of conservation of mass-energy.

simple tools such as wedges, levers, and pulleys to complex devices such as automobiles—use mechanical energy to do work.

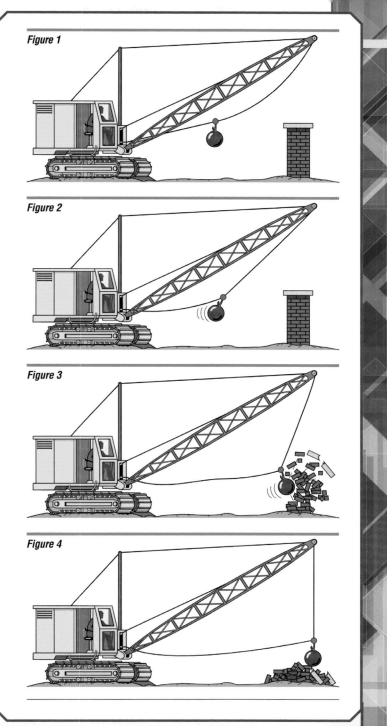

Figure 1 shows stored potential energy in the wrecking ball. Figure 2 shows kinetic energy as the ball swings. Figure 3 shows energy doing work as the ball exerts force against the wall. Figure 4 shows the work done. Encyclopædia Britannica, Inc.

A hammer uses mechanical energy to drive a nail into a board. When raised above the nail, the hammer has potential energy from the work done in lifting it. When the hammer is moved toward the nail, the potential energy becomes part of the kinetic energy that does the work of driving the nail. (The other part comes from work done by muscles in the arm and hand.) Contact between the hammer and the nail transfers energy to the nail and then to the board.

FORMS OF ENERGY

The many forms of energy include chemical, nuclear, electrical, radiant, and heat energy. All these types of energy can do work. Each of these forms can be described as either potential or kinetic energy.

CHEMICAL ENERGY

When several chemicals are mixed together to form gunpowder or dynamite, a violent explosion can occur if care is not taken to prevent this. An explosion can do work against the force of gravity, for example, by throwing pieces of material into the air. A mixture of chemicals that can do work is said to have chemical energy. But not all chemical systems that can do work are as dramatically energetic as gunpowder or dynamite.

Chemical energy can be considered a form of microscopic potential ("stored") energy. Chemical energy is stored in the bonds of chemical compounds and may be released during a chemical reaction, when the compounds are changed.

To understand chemical energy, it is necessary to study what happens during a chemical reaction. Chemical energy is what holds the atoms in a molecule together.

For example, one kind of atom is the oxygen atom (O). An oxygen atom and two hydrogen atoms (H_2) combine to form a water molecule (H_2O). One kind of sand molecule—silicon dioxide (SiO_2)—contains one atom of silicon (Si) and two atoms of oxygen.

Molecules are formed in chemical reactions. Some molecules give off a great deal of energy when they are formed. Such molecules are very stable because all that energy must be put back into them before they break apart. Other molecules release very little energy when they are formed. Such molecules are very unstable. They react easily to form more stable molecules. During these reactions, much energy is given off. Nitroglycerin—a

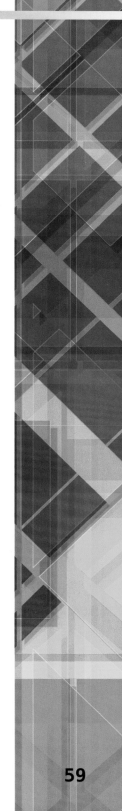

dense, oily liquid—changes readily to water, carbon dioxide, nitrogen, and oxygen. This reaction is explosive because it occurs very rapidly and the suddenly formed gases take up much more room than did the liquid nitroglycerin. Other chemical reactions can produce energy but not be explosive. They may occur more slowly, and the resulting molecules may take up the same amount of room as the original molecules.

Food energy is a form of chemical energy. Plants absorb energy from sunlight and store it in energy-rich chemicals, such as glucose. This process is called photosynthesis. Animals that eat plants use the chemicals created by photosynthesis to maintain life processes. Other animals may eat plant-eating animals to gain the energy-rich chemicals that the plant-eaters formed from the chemicals of plants. Since food energy is what keeps living things moving, it is clearly able to do work.

This giraffe will convert the chemical energy of its food into mechanical energy and heat energy.
J. Nunag/Flickr/Getty Images

Lightning during a thunderstorm is an example of electrical energy. It is the visible exchange of atmospheric electricity. As lightning heats the air, it creates a shock wave that causes the sound of thunder. JanJar/iStock/Thinkstock

Metals are made up of atoms that contain many electrons. Because of the peculiar structure of metal atoms, the atomic nuclei are not strong enough to hold on to all their electrons. Some of the electrons more or less float from nucleus to nucleus. These free electrons can take part in an electric current.

Work must be done to separate negative and positive charges if one is to produce a surplus of electrons in one place and of nuclei that are missing one or more electrons in another place.

When this situation occurs, as in a battery, energy is stored. One end of a metal wire may be connected to the place where excess electrons are collected (the negative terminal on a battery). The other end of the wire is then connected to the place where excess electron-deficient nuclei are collected (the positive terminal on a battery). The electrons in the wire flow to join the nuclei. Electrons farther down the wire flow after the first electrons, and the electrons from the battery move into the wire. The total electron flow from the negative terminal of the battery through the wire and into the positive terminal is an electric current. Since a force is applied that makes the electrons move a certain distance down the wire, work is done.

Magnetic energy is closely related to electrical energy. Magnetic fields are set up whenever electric charges move.

RADIANT ENERGY

Radiant energy is the energy transmitted by electromagnetic radiation. Light is one type of electromagnetic radiation. Other types of electromagnetic radiation include X-rays, radio waves, and microwaves. Radiant energy travels in waves. It can travel through empty space, air, or even solid substances. Radiant energy

CHAPTER 4

MATTER AND ENERGY TOGETHER

Basic ideas about matter trace back to Aristotle, an ancient Greek philosopher with a lifelong interest in the study of the natural world. His writing included examinations of what he perceived to be the fundamental nature of matter and motion. Much later, Newton's three laws of motion described the relations of forces acting on matter to create motion. From its beginnings, scientists understood that matter and energy were interrelated, but it was not until Einstein's theories that science understood how deep that relationship went.

MASS AND ENERGY

For hundreds of years, scientists thought that matter and energy were completely different from each other. But early in the 20th century, Albert Einstein concluded that matter and energy were

closely related. He realized that matter (as mass) could change to energy and energy could change to mass. Einstein described the relationship between mass and energy quantitatively in the famous equation $E = mc^2$. In this equation, E stands for energy, m for mass, and c for the speed of light (which is a constant). The change in mass that is given by this equation is $m = E/c^2$. Since c^2 is a very large quantity, E must be very large indeed for m to be observable. This relationship has been experimentally confirmed.

The Conversion of Matter to Energy

| proton (1.007277 amu) | + | proton (1.007277 amu) | + | neutron (1.008665 amu) | + | neutron (1.008665 am. |

Chemical and nuclear reactions both involve a change in energy linked with a change in mass. Both may involve a reaction in which two entities form two new entities. In a chemical reaction, the entities are atoms or molecules. In a nuclear reaction, they are nuclei. In both cases, the reaction may end up with a loss of mass. This loss is converted to energy, usually in the form of the kinetic energy of the two new entities.

In a chemical reaction, each particle may gain up to 10 eV (electron volts) of energy. This

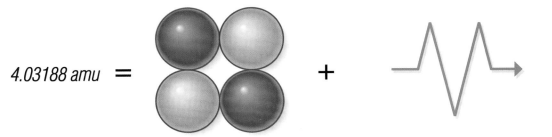

$$4.03188 \text{ amu} \quad = \qquad + $$

helium nucleus
(4.0017 amu)

energy
(equivalent to 0.0302 amu)

The sum of masses of two protons and two neutrons is 4.03188 atomic mass units (amu). When they are joined in a helium nucleus, their mass is 0.0302 amu smaller. The difference has been converted into energy. The helium nucleus is very stable. Encyclopædia Britannica, Inc.

corresponds to a loss of about 10^{-31} grams of mass from each particle, an extremely small amount. If 12 grams (almost half an ounce) of carbon were involved in the reaction, the loss of mass would still be tiny—only 10^{-8} grams. For this reason, the conversion of mass to energy in chemical reactions was not noticed by chemists.

In a nuclear reaction, the energy produced per particle is usually more than 1 MeV (million electron volts). The loss in mass is about a million times larger than the loss in chemical reactions and is readily observable. Nuclear physicists routinely take account of the conversion of mass to energy in their study of nuclear reactions. However, the only difference between the loss of mass in chemical and nuclear reactions is a difference of magnitude. The source of both chemical and nuclear reactions is the same: the transformation of a certain amount of mass into energy.

THE CHANGING FORMS OF ENERGY

One of the most useful properties of energy is that it can be changed from one form to another. These changes are happening all the time. Most machines have as their purpose the conversion of energy from one form to another. Furthermore, even in ordinary activities, energy changes form. A person opening a door uses chemical energy stored in muscle tissues. This energy is converted to the mechanical energy of the moving muscle (as well as to heat energy). The muscle applies a force—a push—to the door and the door swings open. If the door bangs against a wall, some of its mechanical energy is changed to sound energy.

Over centuries of scientific observation, scientists have noticed that energy seems to act in certain uniform ways. A regularity exists in its behavior to which no exceptions have been observed. This regularity has been expressed in the law of the conservation of energy. The law asserts that the total energy of an isolated system does not change. The energy can be redistributed or can change from one form to another, but the total energy remains the same. When a system is not isolated, however, outside forces are able to act on it. In such instances, any change in the energy of the system must exactly equal the work done on it by the outside forces.

The law of the conservation of energy is remarkable because it states that a certain numerical quantity is unchanged throughout

Changing Forms of Energy

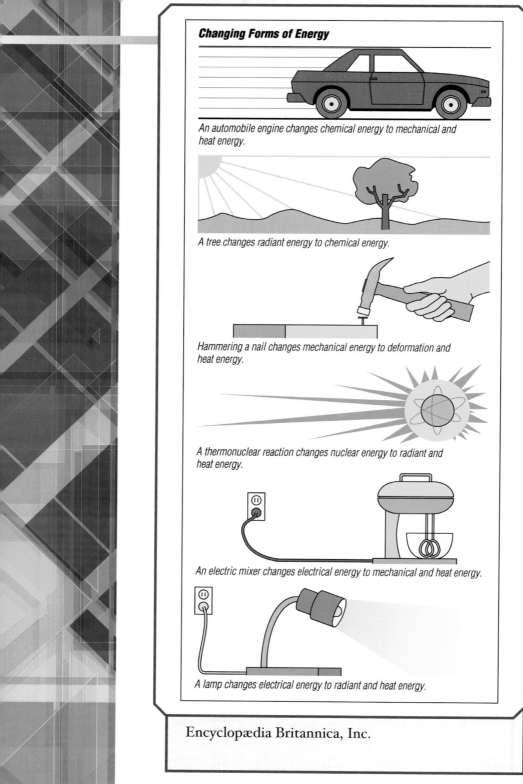

An automobile engine changes chemical energy to mechanical and heat energy.

A tree changes radiant energy to chemical energy.

Hammering a nail changes mechanical energy to deformation and heat energy.

A thermonuclear reaction changes nuclear energy to radiant and heat energy.

An electric mixer changes electrical energy to mechanical and heat energy.

A lamp changes electrical energy to radiant and heat energy.

Encyclopædia Britannica, Inc.

all processes. It does not say why or how this happens. It just says that while the forms of energy are constantly changing, energy itself can neither appear out of nowhere nor vanish into nowhere. Despite the great diversity of energy forms, scientists were able to establish that an amount of one kind of energy has exact equivalents in the other kinds of energy.

What makes the law of the conservation of energy so remarkable is that most of the other quantities that physicists measure are not necessarily conserved. Velocities, accelerations, temperatures, and chemical units, such as atoms and molecules, are not always conserved. However, the amount of matter in a system, like the amount of energy, is also conserved unless some of the matter is changed to energy or some of the energy is changed to matter. To take account of such changes, the law of the conservation of energy is combined with the law of the conservation of mass to form an expanded law of the conservation of mass-energy.

The simplest examples of the conservation of energy are provided by systems in which only mechanical forces are acting. A swinging pendulum, such as the monkey swinging on the vine in the rainforest, continually interchanges kinetic and potential energy. At

the top of the swing, the velocity is zero and the energy is purely potential. At the bottom of the swing, the energy is purely kinetic. In intermediate positions, the energy is partly potential and partly kinetic. However, the sum of the kinetic and the potential energy—the mechanical energy—is constant throughout.

Actually, very few examples exist of purely mechanical systems. A pendulum does not keep on swinging forever. After a while the swings get smaller, and eventually they stop. This happens because the mechanical energy of the pendulum is changed to heat energy by friction. Friction changes mechanical energy to heat energy whenever two pieces of matter move against one another—such as when a person rubs his hands together to warm them.

The motion of the pendulum is slowed by the friction it experiences when it moves through the air and rubs against the hook that holds it up. The energy of the pendulum is transferred to the molecules of the air through which it moves and to the molecules of the hook. The molecules move faster, and the temperature of the air and the hook rises slightly. Mechanical energy has been changed to heat energy.

Friction plays a role in most mechanical situations. It may change some or all of the mechanical energy of the system to heat energy. For example, if a nail is driven into a wall, the work done by the hammer goes into energy of deformation (the nail changes the form of the wall as it moves through it) and into a large amount of heat. The nail and the head of the hammer grow hot.

THE LAWS OF THERMODYNAMICS

In the early 19th century the Industrial Revolution was well underway. The many newly invented machines of the time were powered by the burning of fuel. These machines provided scientists with a great deal of information about how heat energy could be converted to other types of energy, how other types of energy could be converted to heat energy, and how heat energy could do work. Some of these observations were condensed into the laws of thermodynamics. (Thermodynamics is the branch of physics that studies relationships between heat energy, other forms of energy, and work.)

The first law of thermodynamics is a mathematical statement of the conservation of energy. This law says that the amount of heat added to a system exactly equals any change in energy of the system, plus all the work done

by the system. The equations derived from the first law of thermodynamics describe three variables: the internal energy of a system, the heat energy added to the system, and the work done by the system on its surroundings.

The practical importance of the first law of thermodynamics is that it shows that the addition of heat to a system enables it to do work. This, by definition, means that heat is a form of energy. When the first law was proposed, many people found it difficult to accept because they did not believe that heat was a form of energy. They thought of it as a mysterious fluid. But the first law did describe the action of heat engines and of many other kinds of heat interactions, so it came to be accepted as valid.

The first law says that the total energy of the universe remains constant. It does not say what kinds of energy can be changed into what other kinds of energy. After many false starts, a principle—the second law of thermodynamics—was worked out that described the kinds of energy conversions that are possible. This law states that conditions within any system tend to change to a condition of maximum disorder. (The amount of disorder in a system is called entropy.) Work must therefore be done from outside the

The entropy, or amount of disorder, in a system tends to a maximum. When two liquids are mixed together, they become disordered as shown in this mixture of oil and water. sa2324/Shutterstock.com

system to impose more order on the system—that is, to decrease its entropy.

The second law of thermodynamics may seem surprising, yet it does describe many common experiences. For example, when someone kicks off his shoes, it is far more likely that they will land not in the closet where they belong but somewhere else. To get them where they belong, the person must exert work. He must pick them up, carry them to the closet, and place them in their proper location.

Heat energy is the most disordered form of energy. (The individual molecules in an object move in random directions.) Therefore, according to the second law, only a fraction of the heat energy available can be converted to useful work. Heat engines can transform some but not all the heat energy available to them into mechanical energy. The rest remains as heat energy whether or not it is needed, wanted, or welcome.

Mechanical energy, on the other hand, can be completely converted to heat energy. This is a significant asymmetry. In both conversions, the total amount of energy is conserved. But the second law of thermodynamics describes a restriction in the direction in which the conversions of energy can take place.

An automobile engine changes the chemical energy of gasoline into heat energy. The heat energy causes the gas to expand and push on a piston, thereby changing the heat energy partially to mechanical energy. Much of the heat energy, however, simply heats up the engine. The mechanical energy of the pistons is transferred to the tires, which push against the road's surface and move the car forward. But some of the energy in the tires is changed to heat energy by friction. In this and in all other processes involving conversions of heat energy to mechanical energy, much of the original heat energy remains.

To illustrate the difference between the second law of thermodynamics and the first, consider a pan of water that is heated by a burner. The first law of thermodynamics would perfectly well allow the water to freeze and the flame of the burner to get hotter, just as long as the total amount of energy remained the same. The second law of thermodynamics asserts that this is impossible. The process must proceed in the direction that transfers heat from the hotter to the colder body. The general direction of all processes occurring in the observed universe is that which increases entropy.

The third law of thermodynamics concerns a temperature called absolute zero. Absolute zero occurs at about −273 °C (−460 °F). At absolute zero, all substances theoretically

ALBERT EINSTEIN

Albert Einstein was one of the greatest physicists of all time. Einstein was born in Ulm, Germany, on March 14, 1879, of Jewish parents. He was a shy and curious child. He attended a rigorous Munich elementary school where he showed an interest in science and mathematics but did poorly in other areas of study. He finished high school and technical college in Switzerland. At age twenty-two, he became a Swiss citizen. In 1903, he married Mileva Marić. They had two sons but were later divorced. He married his widowed cousin Elsa in 1919.

Between 1909 and 1914, Einstein taught theoretical physics in Switzerland and Germany. Worldwide fame came to him in 1919, when the Royal Society of London announced that predictions made in his general theory of relativity had been confirmed. He was awarded the Nobel Prize for Physics two years later; however, the prize was for his work in theoretical physics, not relativity theories, which were still considered to be controversial.

Beginning in the 1920s, Einstein tried to establish a mathematical relationship between electromagnetism and gravitation. He spent the rest of his life on this unsuccessful attempt to explain all the properties of matter and energy in a single mathematical formula.

Einstein spoke out frequently against nationalism, the exalting of one nation above all others. He opposed war and violence and supported Zionism, the movement to establish a Jewish homeland in Palestine. When the Nazis came to power in Germany in 1933, they denounced his ideas, seized his property, and burned his books. That year, he moved to the United States. In 1940, he became an American citizen.

In 1939, shortly before the outbreak of World War II in Europe, Einstein learned that two German chemists had split the uranium atom. Enrico Fermi, an Italian physicist who lived in the United States, proposed that a chain-reaction splitting of uranium atoms could release enormous quantities of energy. That same year, Einstein wrote to President Franklin D. Roosevelt warning him that this scientific knowledge could lead to Germany's development of an atomic bomb. He suggested that the United States begin preparations for its own atomic bomb research. Einstein's urging led to the creation of the Manhattan Project and the development of the first two atomic bombs in 1945. Einstein died in Princeton, N.J., on April 18, 1955.

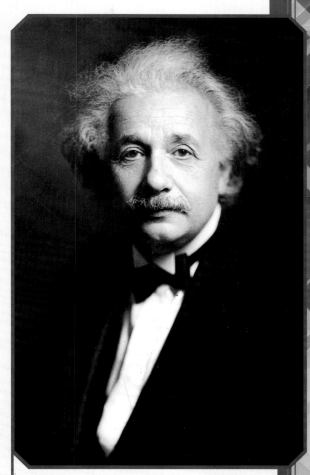

Physicist and mathematician Albert Einstein won the Nobel Prize for Physics in 1921. Popperfoto/Getty Images

would possess the minimum possible amount of energy, and some substances would possess zero entropy (be completely ordered). The third law states that, while absolute zero may be approached more and more closely, it is impossible actually to reach it.

EQUIVALENCE OF MATTER AND ENERGY

Albert Einstein's special theory of relativity, which considers matter and energy equivalent, greatly extended scientists' understanding of matter. This theory states that anything having energy has mass and that the amount of a body's mass (m) is related to the amount of its energy (E). The exact relationship is given by Einstein's famous equation, $E = mc^2$, where c is the speed of light—186,300 miles per second (3×10^8 meters per second).

Scientists had been accustomed to viewing matter and energy as two separate quantities of the universe. But the special theory of relativity relates the two. According to this theory, an object's mass varies as its speed changes. An object traveling at a high velocity will have a greater mass than the same object traveling at a low velocity. The smallest mass a body can have is the mass it has when it is at rest. This minimum mass is called the body's rest mass, and it never changes.

Even at speeds that are ordinarily regarded as quite high—the speed of a jet aircraft, for example—the increase in mass from the rest mass is too small to detect. But in high-energy particle accelerators, when a particle travels at speeds near the speed of light, the mass of the particle increases observably.

Centuries of experiments had also led scientists to believe that the amount of matter in the universe never changes. They expressed this concept as the law of the conservation of mass: matter can neither be created nor destroyed. Similar to this law is the law of the conservation of energy, which states that energy can neither be created nor destroyed. One reason why Einstein's special theory of relativity was so hard to accept was that it said these laws were wrong, that energy can be converted to matter and that matter can be converted to energy. Experimental observations have since confirmed this fact.

The conversion of matter to energy can be demonstrated in nuclear reactions. The masses of individual protons and neutrons are frequently measured in atomic mass units (amu). One amu is $\frac{1}{12}$ of the mass of an atom of carbon-12 (the most common form of carbon).

The mass of a free proton is 1.007277 amu. The mass of a free neutron is slightly larger: 1.008665 amu. When two protons and two neutrons join to form a helium nucleus, one might expect that the mass of the helium nucleus would be equal to the sum of the masses of two protons and two neutrons, or 4.0319 amu. But experiments show that a helium nucleus has a mass of 4.0017 amu, or 0.0302 less than their sum. Scientists theorized that the missing 0.0302 amu had been converted to energy. (See image on pages 72-73.)

The helium nucleus has less energy than its isolated components. That energy difference contributes to the stability of the helium nucleus and is called its binding energy. The exact amount of energy that was given up in forming the helium nucleus must be supplied to break it up, that is, to overcome the binding energy. Scientists can convert between values for mass and values for energy. Thus, 1 amu is equal to 931 MeV (million electron volts), or 1.49×10^{-3} ergs.

Matter changes to energy in chemical reactions, when atoms or molecules are formed, as well as in nuclear reactions. For example, when a hydrogen atom is formed by the combination of a proton and an electron, the mass of the resulting hydrogen atom is less than the sum of the masses of the isolated electron and proton. In this case, however, the mass lost is tiny—only about 2.4×10^{-32} grams, or 1.5×10^{-8} amu. For this reason, the loss of matter during chemical reactions is not observed.

Experiments have convinced scientists that mass and energy are equivalent and interchangeable. The laws of the conservation of mass and the conservation of energy have therefore been combined into a single law, the law of the conservation of mass-energy. This states that the sum of the mass and the energy in the universe is a constant. Transformations between mass and energy are governed by the equation $E = mc^2$.

CHAPTER 5

DIFFERENT THEORIES IN PHYSICS

Where matter and energy meet, scientists observed some problems. Classical physics, the body of physics developed until about the turn of the 20th century, cannot account for the behavior of matter and light at extremely small scales. Scientists have increasingly developed techniques to probe ever more deeply into the structure of matter and to break down matter into its most basic elements. The concept of the atom has existed since the 5th century BCE, but it was not until the beginning of the 19th century that this concept was developed into a scientific theory. Almost as soon as the modern atomic theory was established in the early 20th century, it was discovered that atoms were not the basic point-like building blocks of matter that were being sought. The branch of physics concerned with atomic and subatomic systems is known as quantum mechanics. However, scientists could not marry the theories of quantum mechanics to Einstein's general theory of relativity, which in itself, superseded Newtonian physics. A new theory, string theory was born to explain how both could work at the same time, though even that proved not to be sufficient. Scientists are still searching for a unified theory that will explain all physical properties and processes while working with the theories that are already in place.

EINSTEIN'S THEORIES REGARDING MOVEMENT, LIGHT, AND RELATIVITY

Among the outstanding advances in science will always stand Albert Einstein's theories of relativity—the problem of how physical laws and measurements change when considered by observers in various states of motion. These theories forced revision of all fundamental thinking about time and space. They brought changes in many statements of natural law, including Isaac Newton's law of gravitation. The theories gave scientists the mathematical framework that they needed for atomic research and for releasing atomic energy.

In 1905, at age 26, Einstein published five major research papers in an important German physics journal. He received a doctorate for the first paper. Publication of the next four papers forever changed mankind's view of the universe. The first one provided

a theory explaining Brownian movement, the zigzag motion of microscopic particles in suspension. Einstein suggested that the movement was caused by the random motion of molecules of the suspension medium as they bounced against the suspended particles.

A second paper laid the foundation for the photon, or quantum, theory of light. In it he proposed that light is composed of separate packets of energy, called quanta or photons, which have some of the properties of particles and some of the properties of waves. The paper redefined the theory of light. It also explained the photoelectric effect, the emission of electrons from some solids when they are struck by light. Television and other inventions are practical applications of Einstein's discoveries.

A third paper, which had its beginnings in an essay he wrote at age 16, contained the special theory of relativity. Einstein showed that time and motion are relative to the observer, if the speed of light is constant and natural laws are the same everywhere in the universe. This paper introduced an entirely new concept.

The fourth paper was a mathematical addition to the special theory of relativity. Here, Einstein presented his famous formula, $E = mc^2$, known as the energy-mass relation. What it says is that the energy (E) inherent in a mass (m) equals the mass multiplied by the velocity of light squared (c^2). The formula shows that a small particle of matter is the equivalent of an enormous quantity of energy. These papers established Einstein's status among the most respected physicists in Europe.

QUANTUM MECHANICS

Classical physics, the body of physics developed until about the beginning of the 20th century, cannot account for the behavior of matter and light at extremely small scales. The branch of physics concerned with atomic and subatomic systems is known as quantum mechanics. Its aim is to account for the properties of molecules and atoms and their even tinier constituents, such as electrons, protons, neutrons, and quarks. Quantum mechanics describes how these particles interact with each other and with light, X-rays, gamma rays, and other forms of electromagnetic radiation.

One of the great ideas of the 20th century, quantum mechanics continues to be at the forefront of advances in physics in the 21st century. In addition to explaining the structure of atoms and the behavior of subatomic

NIELS BOHR

Niels Henrik David Bohr was born in Copenhagen, Denmark, on Oct. 7, 1885. His father was a professor of physiology at the University of Copenhagen, and young Bohr grew up among scientists. He entered the university in 1903, winning in 1907 the gold medal of the Royal Danish Academy of Sciences and Letters for his experiments with the vibrations of water to determine its surface tensions.

In 1911, Bohr went to England to study with J. J. Thomson and Ernest Rutherford. His first great work began with a study of the theoretical implications of the nuclear model of the atom proposed by Rutherford. In 1913, he combined the concept of the nuclear atom with the quantum theory of Max Planck and Albert Einstein, departing radically from classical physics. He returned to Copenhagen in 1916 as a professor at the

Niels Bohr's work was a departure from classical physics. He won the Nobel Prize for Physics in 1922, a year after Einstein. George Grantham Bain Collection/Library of Congress, Washington, D.C. (digital file no. LC-DIG-ggbain-35303)

university, becoming director in 1920 of the university's Institute for Theoretical Physics, to which he attracted world-renowned physicists. In 1922, he won the Nobel Prize for Physics for his work on atomic structure.

When Bohr visited the United States early in 1939, he brought with him the knowledge that German scientists had succeeded in splitting the uranium atom. Bohr worked during the winter of 1939–40 at Princeton University, where he developed the theory of atomic fission that led directly to the first atomic bomb. He returned to Denmark in 1940.

After the Germans occupied his country, Bohr was active in the anti-Nazi resistance movement. Under threat of arrest because of his Jewish ancestry, he escaped by fishing boat to Sweden in 1943. He was then flown secretly to England. In the United States, he was an adviser on the atomic bomb project but did not remain to see the first test bomb exploded. In 1957, he received the first U.S. Atoms for Peace Award. He died in Copenhagen on Nov. 18, 1962. Bohr's essays were collected in *Atomic Theory and the Description of Nature* (1934); *Atomic Physics and Human Knowledge* (1958); and *Essays, 1958–1962, on Atomic Physics and Human Knowledge* (1963). His son, Aage Bohr, was a joint winner of the Nobel Prize for Physics in 1975 for his own work on atomic structure.

particles, it has explained the nature of chemical bonds, the properties of crystalline solids, nuclear energy, and the forces that stabilize

collapsed stars. Quantum theory also led directly to the invention of the laser, the electron microscope, and the transistor.

Quantum mechanics has revealed that matter and radiation behave much differently at extremely small scales than at the larger, familiar scales of the everyday world—the world described by classical physics. At atomic scales, the behavior of matter and radiation can seem unusual or downright bizarre. The concepts of quantum mechanics often conflict with common-sense notions, notions that have of course been developed through observations of the world at larger scales. Danish physicist Niels Bohr famously said that "anybody who is not shocked by this subject has failed to understand it."

While the laws of classical physics allow one to determine exactly how matter and radiation will behave, quantum mechanics deals only in probabilities. Indeterminacy—randomness or uncertainty—is fundamental to quantum mechanics. Nevertheless, the success of this field is indisputable. Using probabilities, quantum mechanics makes very precise predictions about the properties of atomic and subatomic systems. In experiments, these predictions have been shown to be extraordinarily accurate—more accurate in fact than those of any other branch of physics.

In the 1800s, physicists had discovered that light behaves like a wave. The German physicist Max Planck proposed the revolutionary quantum theory of light in 1900, in what he called an "act of desperation," to account for certain mysterious facts about the emission of light. He proposed that, rather than being emitted continuously, light can be given off only in tiny bundles, or certain specific amounts of energy, which he called quanta (singular: quantum). Albert Einstein used this quantum theory to explain the photoelectric effect in 1905, proposing that in some ways light behaves like a particle. In the 1920s, Louis-Victor de Broglie extended this idea to matter, proposing that electrons and other "particles" can behave like a wave. This has been confirmed in experiments. Radiation and matter sometimes have characteristics of waves and sometimes have characteristics of particles; they cannot be said to be one or the other.

Among the most important developers of quantum mechanics were Niels Bohr, Erwin Schrödinger, Max Born, and Werner Heisenberg. In 1913, Bohr used the quantum theory to develop a new model of the structure of atoms. In 1926, Schrödinger developed

MAX PLANCK

Max Karl Ernst Ludwig Planck was born on April 23, 1858, in Kiel, Germany. His father, a distinguished jurist and professor of law, taught at the University of Kiel. At the age of nine, Planck entered Munich's famous Maximilian Gymnasium, where a teacher, Hermann Müller, first stimulated his interest in physics and mathematics. Although Planck excelled in all subjects, he decided to pursue a career in physics over his other great love, music.

In 1874, Planck enrolled at the University of Munich but spent a year at the University of Berlin studying with physicists Hermann von Helmholtz and Gustav Robert Kirchhoff. He returned to Munich to work on the second law of thermodynamics and received his doctorate in 1879. The next year, he became a lecturer at the University of Munich and in 1885 was appointed associate professor at Kiel. Four years later, Planck received an appointment to the University of Berlin, where he soon was promoted to full professor of theoretical physics. He remained in Berlin until shortly before his death.

Planck's work on the second law of thermodynamics eventually led to his quantum theory formulations, now known as Planck's radiation law and Planck's constant (symbolized by h). Planck's radiation law is a mathematical relationship calculated to measure the radiation of energy by a blackbody, or perfectly radiating object. In formulating the law, Planck had to abandon one of his most cherished beliefs—that the second law of thermodynamics was an absolute law of nature. Instead, he had to accept the fact that the second law is a statistical law. In addition, Planck had to assume in his formulations that radiation is emitted, transmitted, and absorbed, not continuously but in discrete packets or quanta of energy.

He also introduced his constant *h* in his radiation law calculations. Planck's constant is the product of energy multiplied by time, a quantity called action, and is often defined as the elementary quantum of action. It is the fundamental physical constant used in mathematical calculations of quantum mechanics, which describes the behavior of particles and waves on the atomic scale.

Planck announced his findings in 1900, but it was years before the full consequences of his revolutionary quantum theory were recognized. Throughout his life, Planck made significant contributions to optics, thermodynamics and statistical mechanics, physical chemistry, and other fields. In 1930, he was elected president of the Kaiser Wilhelm Society, which was renamed the Max Planck Society after World War II. Though deeply opposed to the fascist regime of Adolf Hitler, Planck remained in Germany throughout the war. He died in Göttingen on Oct. 4, 1947.

Max Planck, pictured here in 1920, gave up music to pursue a career in physics. Science and Society/ SuperStock

the fundamental mathematical equation of quantum mechanics. It is radically different from Isaac Newton's laws of motion, which are fundamental to classical physics, in that it indicates only probabilities. The solutions to the Schrödinger equation are wave functions, and Born showed that these functions can indicate the likelihood that a certain particle will be in a given place at a given time. According to Heisenberg's famous uncertainty principle of 1927, it is impossible to measure both the exact position of a particle and its exact velocity at a given moment—even in theory. The more accurately one measures the position, the less accurately one can measure the velocity, and vice versa. The concepts of exact position and exact velocity together, in fact, have no meaning in nature.

STRING THEORY

Relativity is essential for studying the universe on a large scale, when extremely high speeds or great densities are involved, and for understanding gravity. On the other hand, the branch of physics known as quantum mechanics studies matter and energy at the smallest scales, including subatomic particles and processes. It has been difficult to fully join the two into one unified framework of physics. In an attempt to develop a unified theory, many physicists have turned to string theory. According to this theory, elementary particles are not dimensionless points but tiny one-dimensional string-like objects. Although these "strings" are so small that they appear to be points, they actually have a tiny length. If one billion trillion trillion of them were laid end to end, they would together be only about 0.4 inch (1 centimeter) long.

According to string theory, these strings make up all matter, and they vibrate. The particular pattern of a string's vibrations corresponds to a particular type of particle. The strings that form electrons all have one vibrational pattern, for instance, while those that form quarks have a different pattern, and photons yet another.

In string theory, the universe is made up of more than the three dimensions of space and the one dimension of time that we observe. Instead, in most versions of the theory, there are eleven dimensions (ten of space and one of time). The extra dimensions are curled up so as to be imperceptible.

String theory was first developed in the 1970s to describe the strong force. The theory became popular in the 1980s, when it was

The Large Hadron Collider (LHC) located in Geneva, Switzerland, is the world's most powerful particle accelerator. The goal of the LHC project is to understand the fundamental nature of matter by re-creating the extreme conditions that occurred in the first few moments of the universe according to the big bang model. Mint Images – Frans Lanting/Getty Images

shown that it might be a way to incorporate all types of matter and all four known fundamental forces, including gravity, into one framework. Such a comprehensive physical theory is known as a unified field theory or a "theory of everything."

Although the mathematics of string theory has shown great promise, the theory has not yet been verified by experiment. Strings, if they exist, are extremely tiny. Physicists hope that the latest generation of particle accelerators will be able to detect such small objects. They are also seeking other ways to confirm string theory. In the meantime, it remains a totally theoretical construct.

CONCLUSION

The study of the physical universe, and all that we understand about matter and energy, has influenced other disciplines in science. In cosmology, discoveries about matter and energy have led to strange discoveries about the universe. The big bang theory presented the idea of an expanding universe to cosmologists, who theorized that the universe is still expanding, but until recently, they believed that the rate of expansion was slowing down. The next question was whether the universe had critical density, a mass density at which the expansion of the universe would slow down to a stop and reverse, like a rubber band snapping back onto itself. But surveys of visible matter fell short, with only about 1 percent of the necessary mass. This led to the theory that there must be unseen matter in the universe, which scientists called dark matter. Scientists returned to an old theory of Einstein's that explained that empty space is not nothing. Einstein's cosmological constant predicted that so-called empty space could contain its own energy. This undetected energy was dubbed "dark energy."

Though much has been discovered throughout human history about the nature of the
universe and its building blocks of matter and
energy, there are still many questions to be
answered. What we know about matter and
energy has changed with the theories of dark
matter and dark energy, and that it comprises
most of what we once thought of as empty
space in the universe, just as an atom is mostly
empty space. The aim of physicists is to recon-
cile the laws of physics as we understand them
on two extremes: on the submicroscopic level
of bosons and leptons, and on the extragalactic level that governs the motion of galaxies.

Rather than nixing previous theories, a new
unified theory would expand on the general
theory of relativity quantum mechanics, and
string theory in a way that explains how these
all work together. Just as Einstein's general
theory of relativity did not make Newtonian
physics wrong, in effect, these separate theories would still apply but be limited in their
application, while the new theory would
go further to explain more of the universe,
explaining how the microscopic and macro-
scopic are governed by the same laws.

GLOSSARY

annihilation The process in which a particle and antiparticle mutually destroy each other.

astronomical Pertaining to materials in the universe beyond Earth's atmosphere.

cataclysmic Pertaining to a sudden and violent physical action.

centripetal force The force that acts upon a body moving along a curved path around a central point.

charged Having a basic property of elementary particles that gives rise to electrical forces and is classified as positive or negative charge.

collision The meeting of two particles that exert force on each other.

decay In nuclear physics, to change spontaneously into one or more different atomic nuclei.

emitting Discharging or releasing.

entropy The degradation of matter and energy into a state of inert uniformity.

extragalactic Originating outside the Milky Way galaxy.

framework A structure of ideas that support something.

fundamental The foundation or basis.

meter The base unit of length in the International System of Units.

oriented Positioned with reference to other points.

phase A particular appearance or state, such as solid, liquid, or gas.

phenomenon In science, an observable event that is of scientific interest to describe and explain.

radioactive Pertaining to unstable atoms that can spontaneously emit nuclear radiation.

submicroscopic Too small to be seen in an ordinary light microscope.

theory An idea or set of ideas that is intended to explain facts or events.

thermal Of, relating to, or caused by heat.

vector A quantity that has both size and direction and can be represented by a line segment in mathematics.

velocity The speed and direction of an object or wave.

volt A units of electrical potential difference and electromotive force, used as a standard of measurement.

American Association for the Advancement
of Science (AAAS)
1200 New York Avenue NW
Washington, DC 20005
(202) 326-6400
Website: http://www.aaas.org
The AAAS board seeks to enhance com-
munication among scientists, engineers,
and the public; promote and defend
the integrity of science and its use;
strengthen and support the science and
technology enterprise; provide a voice
for science on societal issues; and promote the responsible use of science in
public policy, among other goals.

American Institute of Physics (AIP)
1 Physics Ellipse
College Park, MD 20740
(301) 209-3100
Website: http://www.aip.org
The American Institute of Physics is a
national society dedicated to the advancement and diffusion of the knowledge
of physics and its application to human
welfare.

American Physical Society (APS)
1 Physics Ellipse
College Park, MD 20740
(301) 209-3200
Website: http://www.aps.org
The goal of APS is to be the leading voice
    for physics and an authoritative source
    of physics information for the advance-
    ment of physics. It also aims to provide
    effective programs in support of the
    physics community.

Canadian Association of Physicists (CAP)
Suite 112, MacDonald Building
University of Ottawa
150 Louis Pasteur Priv.
Ottawa, ON K1N 6N5
Canada
(613) 562-5614
Website: http://www.cap.ca
Established in 1945, the Canadian Association
    of Physicists highlights the achievements
    in Canadian physics research and pursues
    policy and education that enhance the
    study of physics.

National Society of Black Physicists (NSBP)
1100 N. Glebe Road, Suite 1010

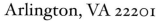

Arlington, VA 22201
(703) 536-4207
Website: http://www.nsbp.org
The mission of the National Society of Black
   Physicists is to promote the professional
   well-being of African American physicists
   and physics students within the international scientific community and society.

Society of Physics Students (SPS)
1 Physics Ellipse
College Park, MD 20740
(301) 209-0839
Website: http://www.spsnational.org
This professional association is explicitly
   designed for students of physics or anyone
   interested in the study of physics. It is also
   the home of Sigma Pi Sigma, the national
   physics honor society.

WEBSITES

Because of the changing nature of Internet
links, Rosen Publishing has developed an
online list of websites related to the subject
of this book. This site is updated regularly.
Please use this link to access the list:

http://www.rosenlinks.com/SCI/Phys

FOR FURTHER READING

Clemens, Nora. *Discovering the Nature of Energy.* New York, NY: Rosen Publishing, 2012.

Cutnell, John D., and Kenneth W. Johnson. *Physics.* 8th ed. Hoboken, NJ: Wiley, 2009.

Ferreira, Pedro G. *The Perfect Theory: A Century of Geniuses and the Battle Over General Relativity.* New York, NY: Houghton Mifflin Harcourt, 2014.

Field, Andrea R., ed. *Energy.* New York, NY: Rosen Publishing, 2012.

Field, Andrea R., ed. *Matter.* New York, NY: Rosen Publishing, 2012.

Gates, Evalyn. *Einstein's Telescope: The Hunt for Dark Matter and Dark Energy in the Universe.* New York, NY: W. W. Norton & Co., 2010.

Gregersen, Erik, ed. *The Britannica Guide to Relativity and Quantum Mechanics.* New York, NY: Rosen Publishing, 2011.

Hawking, Stephen. *A Brief History of Time.* New York, NY: Bantam, 1998.

Matter and Energy. Nashua, NH: Delta Education, 2010.

Panek, Richard. *The 4 Percent Universe: Dark Matter, Dark Energy, and the Race to Discover the Rest of Reality.* New York, NY: Houghton Mifflin Harcourt, 2011.

INDEX